Lessons Learned

Reflections on Life's Journey

SUZETTE B. BACUS

Table of Contents

Father's Protective Love: Shaping Childhood Memories

BY: SUZETTE B. BACUS

In my childhood's recollection,
Father's conservatism shaped our protection.
Sleepovers at friends were not permitted,
To shield us from perils, he insisted.

I recall my dear grandmother's plea,
To spend one night in her company.
Yearning to feel her embrace so tight,
My father agreed, albeit just for one night.

For his love for his mother was immense,
Their bond is a precious inheritance.
"Dresses won't do," my father advised,
Opting for pants, was a choice that was wise.

He wanted us comfortable in every stance,
Free to explore, leap, and dance.
Father's concern, in his unique way,
Ensured our safety day after day.

Embracing the Comedy of Farting

By: Suzette B. Baluarte

When the initial flatulence is released,
It's the one who dealt it, soon deceased.
Farting, a peculiar phenomenon, indeed,
Amusing some, while others feel the need.

In my loyal friend, a bond I find,
Laughter shared, no offense behind.
When gas escapes, worries dissolve,
Boundaries blurred, we evolve.

Farting, at times, becomes a jest,
Eliciting looks, both clean and in jest.
For in its wake, a follow-up awaits,
An inevitable sequence, comedy's traits.

This bodily function, good for health,
Releases gas, a benefit in stealth.
No one can evade its timely call,
A better life, we embrace it all.

Navigating Life's Journey with a Digital Atlas

By: Suzette B. Bacus

In a new town, seeking my way,
Yearning for guidance, day by day.
My phone becomes an atlas, my reliable aid,
Leading me to where I'll be safely laid.

On the right path, assurance abounds,
Yet doubts may linger, and their whispers resound.
But I continue to read my digital guide,
Ensuring swift navigation, with nothing to hide.

Thanks to technology's rapid advance,
The atlas is a mere click, a fortunate chance.
No longer bound to buying maps of yore,
Convenience at hand, forevermore.

With GPS precision, I venture with ease,
Exploring new horizons, guided by these.
No need to fumble with cumbersome maps,
The atlas on my phone, a traveler's collapse.

So I embrace this modern age's grace,
Where technology streamlines my journey's pace.
From town to town, my atlas Junfolds,
A digital companion, navigating roads untold.

The Delightful Power of Yogurts

By: Suzette B. Bacus

Yogurts, how I adore your delectable taste,
Nourishing my body, a healthy embrace.
A snack so versatile, you never disappoint,
Satisfying cravings, each delightful joint.

Recommended for kids, a wholesome treat,
Nutrition-packed, making meals complete.
Low in calories, yet bursting with might,
Yogurts, a superstar, shining so bright.

Oh, the wonders you hold, a nutrient treasure,
Supporting well-being, beyond measure.
Digestive health you fortify and restore,
With each creamy spoonful, I adore you more.

From calcium to probiotics, a nutritional delight,
Yogurts, you're a powerhouse, day and night.
For all the health benefits you provide,
Incorporating you into my diet, I take in stride

Embracing Life's Second Chance with Gratitude and Purpose

By: Suzette B. Bacus

In moments of despair, as I stumbled and fell,
Thoughts of life's end within me would dwell.
But a guardian angel led me to a clinic's care,
A touch of magic, divine love in the air.

Fourteen treacherous stairs seemed to harm,
Yet God's warm embrace kept me from the alarm.
He shielded me from tragedy's cruel grasp,
For a mission awaited, a purpose to clasp.

My second life, a remarkable gift bestowed,
Each moment is cherished, its value bestowed.
Every breath is worth sharing with those in need,
Extending compassion to the deprived, indeed.

Two nights, three days in the hospital's embrace,
A profound realization, life's vibrant grace.
Not solely for my family's tender embrace,
But also, for my students, a guiding space.

Each person we encounter, their tale unique,
Their journeys diverge, and the destinies they seek.
In God's hands, trust firmly placed above,
For He reigns supreme, the source of boundless love.

Embracing Life's Journey with Faith, Love, and Hope

BY: SUZETTE B. BACUS

In God's eyes, we're truly unique,
Given time to forgive, our souls to cleanse and seek.
With faith, love, and hope, we stand,
From dust we arise, into dust, we expand.

God's trust in us is profound,
Guiding us to do what's right, bound.
Creating a better world, a place to thrive,
Following His path, happiness shall arrive.

Life, a journey with a starting point,
An endpoint where we shall disjoint.
Yet, if we follow His divine decree,
True joy and fulfillment, we shall see.

Life's journey begins with a sacred breath,
And concludes as we face the realm of death.
By following His path, we find our way,
Discovering true happiness day by day.

The Noble Journey of the Military

By: Suzette B. Bacus

In the realm of valor, they proudly stand,
With an unwavering dedication to their homeland.
Leaving behind their loved ones, they answer the call,
To serve their country, giving it their all.

Men and women of honor, a mighty force,
Endowed with power, a noble discourse.
Some belong to the army, strong and true,
Guarding the land, for freedom they pursue.

Others take to the seas, ships, and boats their domain,
The brave navy men, their duty never in vain.
And there are those who soar high above,
Airmen, masters of the sky they prove.

In their selfless service, a nation finds pride,
These heroes united, standing side by side.
They sacrifice, they protect, they bravely defend,
The military's noble journey, that will end

Embracing Opportunities and Summer's Delights

By: Suzette B. Bacus

Seize the day when the iron glows bright,
Opportunities beckon, igniting delight.
Amidst my favorites, you shine so true,
Like a blazing bratwurst, sizzling through.

Strike while the iron is hot, don't delay,
As pork sisig sizzles, its allure is at play.
A delectable delight, pleasing to the taste,
Quenching my hunger with flavors embraced.

Embrace the fervor, let passion ignite,
As summer draws near, a vibrant sight.
A season of laughter, adventure untold,
Where joy and excitement take hold.

Bask in the sun, with endless delight,
Embrace the warmth, from morning till night.
In summer's embrace, life comes alive,
With thrills and fun, let your spirit thrive.

Finding Strength and Faith Amidst Adversity

By: Suzette B. Bacus

In a chapter of my life, I recall,
Where kindness prevailed overall.
Yet, despite my earnest endeavors,
Detractors emerged, like relentless thorns.

Such instances bring painful strife,
But I confront them, embracing the challenge of life.
Not to prove or disprove their claims,
But to glean positivity from the flames.

When efforts go unseen, unrecognized,
Truth shall prevail, unmasked and prized.
Always bear in mind, never forget,
That in times of anguish, God's presence is set.

For the forsaken, persecuted, and in pain,
Divine solace shall accompany their terrain.
Hold onto faith, for it shall sustain,
In the face of trials, resilience will reign.

My Journey as an Accidental Teacher

By: Suzette B. Bacus

In the midst of an intriguing day,
Jesus transformed my story, I must say.
An accidental teacher, a role unforeseen,
With a whiteboard and marker, I became keen.

Passion surged within, a calling in my heart,
To share knowledge and wisdom is my cherished part.
Gifted by God, entrusted with this task,
To guide and inspire, an important ask.

Follow your heart, let fear be released,
For faith shall guide you, providing inner peace.
Embrace consequences with an obedient stride,
Making a difference, with purpose as our guide.

My journey unfolded, a path newly paved,
A teacher I became, lives to be saved.
Through lessons and discussions, I sought to impart,
The beauty of learning, igniting minds and hearts.

With patience and care, I fostered their growth,
Nurturing curiosity, allowing minds to both wander and troth.
In each student's eyes, I witnessed the spark,
As they embraced knowledge, lighting up the dark.

Challenges emerged, trials to face,
But with faith as my compass, I found my place.
Knowing that within me, a higher power resides,
Guiding my steps, as I journeyed on tides.
The impact I had, not measured in grades,
But in the transformation, in the paths they paved.
Empowering young minds, encouraging dreams,
Unleashing their potential, like flowing streams.

From the depths of my soul, I knew it to be true,
That teaching was my calling, my purpose to pursue.
To shape lives, to make a lasting impression,
To inspire and guide, with unwavering passion.

So, follow your heart, embrace your calling with zeal,
For in obedience, the path becomes real.
May we make a difference, in every life we touch,
Spreading love and wisdom, as we journey much.

In the tapestry of education, may we weave,
A tapestry of hope, where dreams can believe.
In teaching and learning, we find the key,
To unlock the potential, that sets spirits free.

A day transformed, a calling fulfilled,
As an accidental teacher, my purpose was distilled.
With gratitude in my heart, I embrace the chance,
To touch lives, making a lasting dance.

Digital Canvas:
Painting Lines of Code

BY: GIBE S. TIROL

On a digital canvas, pristine and bright,
Lines of code weave, in the realm of byte.
A painter's brush transformed, with keystrokes bold,
Creating artistry, where stories unfold.

With syntax as the palette, colors unseen,
Programmers become artists, in the virtual scene.
Each line a stroke, carefully placed,
Building a masterpiece, interlaced.

The canvas expands, a boundless space,
Where imagination runs, in a coding chase.
From variables to functions, the elements blend,
Bringing life to the canvas, from beginning to end.
Loops dance gracefully, in elegant swirls,
As if brushstrokes, creating patterns that unfurl.
Conditionals paint depth, adding shades of choice,
Guiding the viewer's gaze, with a confident voice.

The code becomes art, as it takes its form,
Transforming ideas, in a digital storm.
Abstract concepts made tangible, for all to see,
A fusion of logic and creativity.

Through algorithms and structures, the canvas sings,
A symphony of bytes, where innovation springs.
The lines of code tell a story profound,
In this digital canvas, a world is found.

So let us paint, with lines of code,
Unleashing creativity, in a digital ode.
For on this canvas, vast and wide,
Limitless possibilities reside.

Social Media Insanity

By: Janeth S. Ugang

In cybersphere, a tale unfolds,
Minds mingled, entwined, and puzzled,
A domain of chaos where stillness screams,
Witness the distraction of social media streams.

Morning arises until the darkness shows,
Tweet of stories on screen it glows,
The desire for likes, a longing of the heart,
Yearning for connections that are out of sight.

Through filtered photos, we paint our lives,
Sparkling lights of glory transcend the drives,
Likes and shares are all we long for,
Hoping it comes, but sadly losing its' galore.

Amidst the network clamor of voices around,
Yet worthless echoes reach the ground,
Family, friends, and the society they surround,
Genuine relationships are buried underground.
In the shadows between reality and virtual blur,
The unceasing yearning of mirroring obscure,
A digital thirst in this unfathomable stream,
Insanity in social media, we chase to be first.

Beyond the glory of endless stream,
A ray of sunshine, a likelihood to redeem,
In the middle of the madness and noise,
Remains the possibility of obtaining real joy.

Two Souls Entwined:
The Journey of Marriage

By: Pet Andrew P. Nacua

In the realm of love, where hearts intertwine,
Lies the complex journey of marriage, a tale unrefined.
Through struggles endured, a union put to the test,
Let these words weave a story, with no duplicate in jest.

Like turbulent seas, marriage faces its storms,
Emotions clash, as resentment takes its forms.
Communication falters, like ships in the night,
Yet hope lingers, seeking a path back to light.

The flame that once burned with passionate desire,
Now flickers weakly, and its warmth begins to tire.
Misunderstandings breed in the shadows of doubt,
But love's ember persists, refusing to snuff out.

In the depths of despair, resentment takes hold,
Seeds of discontent, once sown, are hard to unfold.
But love's resilience, a force to be reckoned with,
Takes root in the cracks, where healing is beckoned.

Patience becomes a bridge to understanding's shore,
Empathy is a balm, the wounds begin to restore.
In vulnerability's embrace, walls start to crumble,
Allowing forgiveness to grow, no longer humbled.

Through tears shed in darkness, a new dawn will rise,
Marriage is a battlefield, where love defies demise.
The battles fought together, with scars that we bear,
Become a testament of strength, a love beyond compare.
For in the struggle lies an opportunity to grow,
To mend what is broken, to reap what we sow.
The dance of compromise, a delicate art,
Weaving threads of unity, binding souls heart to heart.

And so we learn, in marriage's arduous quest,
In the midst of struggles, we find what is best.
For it's through overcoming, we emerge refined,
Stronger than before, with hearts intertwined.

No two stories are alike, each one stands alone,
Marriage's struggles are uniquely etched in stone.
But through commitment and unwavering grace,
Love's flame rekindles, embracing a newfound space.

So let us cherish the journey, with its ebb and flow,
Embrace the struggles, for they help us to grow.
For in the unique tapestry of marital strife,
We discover the depths of love, and its power to truly thrive.

Tapestry of Life

By: Pet Andrew P. Nacua

22

Life's tapestry unfolds, a canvas of diverse hues,
Each experience is unique, with no duplicates to choose from.
Through triumph and trial, we navigate the unknown,
In this grand journey, our stories are beautifully sewn.

A child's first steps, a moment filled with glee,
A milestone in time, pure innocence set free.
The taste of victory, the sweet fruits of success,
The culmination of efforts, a feeling we caress.

Heartbreak's embrace, a lesson learned so deep,
A shattered soul, in tears we silently weep.
But from the fragments, resilience finds its way,
We rise from ashes, more vital day by day.

The thrill of adventure, the world as our stage,
Uncharted territories, where dreams engage.
With every new horizon, we broaden our sight,
Embracing the unknown, in pursuit of delight.
A sunset's embrace, painting the sky's embrace,
Nature's symphony, where serenity finds its place.
In quiet moments, we find solace and peace,
A reminder of life's wonders, a blessed release.

Friendships forged, bonds that time cannot sever,
Kindred spirits, with hearts united forever.
Laughter shared, memories etched in our core,
The love of companionship is a treasure we adore.

Lessons from elders, wisdom's cherished gift,
Their stories are a tapestry of experience and uplift.
Their counsel guides us, as we tread our way,
Their legacy lives on, with every step we convey.

Life's surprises, unexpected twists and turns,
Opportunities are discovered, where passion brightly burns.
In the dance of luck, we find our purpose true,
A calling that ignites, as our dreams come into view.

So let us cherish the uniqueness of our path,
Embrace the mosaic of moments, in love's aftermath.
For in the tapestry of life, no duplicates are found,
Our experiences shape us, in their beauty unbound.

SHORT STORY

How I Transformed Lives as an Idol

By: Suzette B. Bacus

I have talked to my nephew just recently. He told me that when he was young, his mom literally talked about me. He said that he does not know me personally as his aunt, but he grows that he knows me already.

Even before he considered me as her "IDOL" because his mom literally emphasized to him that "Poverty is not the hindrance of success in life". As their model without personally knowing me, they were motivated to do their part to become successful. And because of that, they are also very eager to know me until I invited them home way back in 2007 and then that was our first encounter which led us to become close friends. Their mom and dad are also like my parents who are FARMERS too.

The story of their parents about me makes them who they are right now. They are seven siblings and become professionals except for their youngest who is now 15 years old.

Some of their courses:

- Computer Science
- Business Administration
- AB Political Science
- 3 Mining Engineer (including him)

To his young and impressionable mind, I became more than just an aunt. Through his mother's anecdotes and words of admiration, I transformed into an "IDOL" in his eyes. His mother consistently emphasized the belief that poverty should never be seen as a hindrance to success in life. Through these powerful messages, I became a symbol of inspiration and a testament to the idea that one's circumstances need not dictate their future. Despite never meeting me, this perception of me as a figure of triumph and possibility motivated him and his siblings to strive for greatness.

They saw firsthand how the principles and values I embodied guided me toward success. These narratives ingrained in them the belief that with determination and dedication, they could overcome any obstacle. The stories became a source of motivation, inspiring them to do their part in the journey toward success.

To think that my own experiences and the values I hold dear played a part in shaping these remarkable individuals fills me with immense joy.

From being regarded as an "IDOL" before even meeting them, to our first encounter that solidified our friendship, to the lasting bonds we have formed as a chosen family, the power of storytelling and the influence we have on others' lives is evident. Through shared experiences, mutual support, and a deep understanding, we have grown together, guided by the principles of hard work, determination, and the belief that poverty should never limit one's aspirations.

Following the Rain, a Rainbow

BY: NOREEN B. FUENTES

Maya was a small girl who lived in a little town at the base of a gigantic mountain. Maya was known for her fierce toughness and unwavering attitude. She had many difficulties and failures, yet she never gave up on her goals.

Maya awakened one bright morning with a raging urge to scale the gorgeous mountain that dominated the village's surroundings. Maya was driven to discover whether the stories were true because it was believed that achieving the top would grant one's greatest dreams.

Maya set off on her expedition with little more than a small knapsack full of provisions and an optimistic heart, undaunted of the daunting struggle that lied ahead. As she continued up the hill, the route in front of her became steeper and more perilous. Maya's resolve was pushed to the test with each move, but she refused to give up.

Maya encountered various challenges on her journey as the days progressed into weeks. She came over steep gorges, slick hills, and raging storms that threatened to throw her back. Maya, though, managed to adjust and move on despite each setback. She asked the locals for advice, absorbed their knowledge, and took strength from their support.

Maya experienced uncertainty and tiredness at several points during her long trek. She frequently wondered if the peak was really within reach and doubted her own ability. But each time she was about to give up, she would recall why she had started.

She remembered her dreams, her goals, and the certainty that had always been a part of her.

Maya struggled for months before reaching the summit. She took in the breathtaking scene in front of her as if she were poised atop the world. In terms of beauty, the sight far surpassed her expectations. Maya had a great feeling of accomplishment and contentment at that very moment. She was well aware that, despite all odds, it had been her unwavering perseverance that had brought her here.

As she made her way down the mountain, Maya gained fresh tenacity and resiliency. She'd realized that perseverance entailed appreciating the journey as much as the result. It was about facing one's fears.

Maya inspired others when she returned to the community. She recounted her experience and emphasized to everyone that tenacity was the key to realizing their own potential. She urged them to have great dreams, to work tirelessly to fulfill their passions, and to never give up on themselves.

Thus, Maya's inspiring story of tenacity persisted and continued to be told across the town for many years. Her steadfast attitude turned into a symbol of optimism, showing everyone that everything was possible if they had the will and the fortitude to pursue it

The Enchanting
Adventures of Snow:
A Tale of Canine Wonder

By: Pet Andrew P. Nacua

Once upon a time, in a cozy little house nestled amidst rolling green hills, lived a delightful dog named Snow. With his fluffy white fur, short nose, and endearing Shih Tzu features, he was a bundle of joy that brought warmth and laughter to everyone he encountered.

Snow's days were filled with endless adventures and wagging tails. He would bound through the meadows, his paws leaving little imprints on the soft grass, as he chased after butterflies that danced in the summer breeze. His playful nature and gentle demeanor made him a cherished companion in the neighborhood, where he quickly became known as the "Fluffy Ambassador of Happiness."

Every morning, Snow would wake up to the aroma of freshly baked treats lovingly prepared by his human, Mary Mae. She would ruffle his fur and shower him with affection, whispering sweet words that made his tail wag uncontrollably. Snow and Mary Mae were inseparable, sharing a bond that words couldn't describe.

One fateful day, as Snow and Mary Mae took their usual stroll through the park, they stumbled upon a lost kitten, shivering and scared. Without hesitation, Snow's compassionate heart urged him to protect and care for the little feline. With gentle nudges and a reassuring presence, he comforted the kitten, who promptly curled up next to Snow's warm and fluffy side.

Mary Mae, touched by Snow's unwavering kindness, decided to take the kitten home and named her Whiskers. From that day forward, Snow and Whiskers became the best of friends, embarking on mischievous adventures and creating a harmonious duo that filled the house with joy and laughter.

Snow and Whiskers would spend their days engaged in playful antics, chasing each other's tails and pouncing on imaginary foes. Together, they transformed the house into a lively playground, leaving a trail of toys and laughter in their wake. Their harmonious friendship brought out the inner child in Mary Mae, who often found herself joining in their games, her heart filled with the purest form of happiness.

As time passed, Snow grew older, his once energetic spirit mellowing into a wise and loving presence. Yet, his love for life remained undiminished. He would spend his days basking in the warmth of the sun, watching over Whiskers as she continued to fill the house with her playful energy. Snow's gentle nature served as a guiding light, instilling in Whiskers the lessons of kindness, compassion, and the importance of unconditional love.

One winter's night, as the snowflakes fell softly from the sky, Snow peacefully passed away, leaving behind a legacy of love and joy that would forever be etched in the hearts of those he touched. Whiskers, now a grown cat, kept Snow's memory alive, embodying the wisdom and kindness she had learned from her dear friend.

In the years that followed, the neighborhood would fondly reminisce about Snow, the fluffy Shih Tzu with the short nose, who had brought so much happiness into their lives. His legacy lived on, reminding everyone that even the smallest of creatures can have the biggest hearts and leave an indelible mark on the world.

And so, the tale of Snow, the fluffy and loving Shih Tzu, serves as a reminder that true happiness can be found in the simplest of things—loyal companionship, unwavering love, and the ability to touch the lives of others. As the seasons change and time goes by, Snow's spirit continues to sprinkle its magic, forever etched in the memories of those who were fortunate enough to know him.